ETOSHA

A VISUAL SOUVENIR

DARYL AND SHARNA BALFOUR

Struik Publishers (Pty) Ltd
(a member of the Struik Publishing Group)
80 McKenzie Street
Cape Town 8001
Reg. No.: 54/00965/07

ISBN 1 86872 045 4

Copyright in published edition:
Struik Publishers (Pty) Ltd 1997
Copyright in text: Daryl & Sharna Balfour 1997
Copyright in photographs: Daryl & Sharna Balfour

Editor: Pippa Parker
Designer: Dean Pollard
Reproduction: cmyk pre-press
Printing: Times Offset (M) Sdn Bhd

Front cover: Elephant herd on the move.

Spine: Lilacbreasted Roller.

Back cover: Mixed herd at water.

Title page: Giraffe, eland and zebra at waterhole.

Right: Lion pride at rest at Okundeka.

INTRODUCTION

Set in the northern part of Namibia, Etosha
National Park is one of Africa's largest game
sanctuaries. It is also one of its finest.
Stretching more than 350 kilometres from east
to west, the park covers a total area of 22 275
square kilometres. This area is dominated by
the expansive Etosha Pan (its name means
'great white place'), once a vast inland sea;
now, for most months of the year, a parched,
salt-encrusted wasteland. Surrounding the pan
are the open grasslands and thorn thickets —
lifeblood of an area which sustains more than
114 mammal and 340 bird species.

Elephants are synonymous with Etosha and are
especially in evidence during the dry season,
when large herds move in to take advantage of
a reliable water supply.

Right: The African wild cat, a nocturnal predator, is similar in appearance to the domestic tabby.

Opposite: Spotted hyaena. The brown hyaena and the aardwolf, a related species, also occur occur in Etosha.

A black rhino caught in motion. All the black rhino found in Namibia are of the subspecies Diceros bicornis bicornis, *the well-known desert rhino found to the west of Etosha in Damaraland and the Kaokoveld. White rhino are also present in the park: they were recently introduced and are reported to be thriving.*

It is only from a height that one can truly appreciate the size of Etosha Pan, which spans an area of more than 6 100 square kilometres. Its flat surface, though barren, is often enlivened by the animals, such as these gemsbok, that make their way across in search of the greener pastures beyond.

Overleaf: Spring flowers, such as these devil's thorn blooms, emerge in splendid abundance after the first spring rains.

Previous page: A herd of elephants moves with purpose along a well-used path to a remote waterhole in the park's southern reaches.

Left: A somewhat startled Spotted Eagle Owl, one of eight owl species found in Etosha.

Right: A pair of Secretary Birds in their roost atop one of the park's flat-topped acacia trees.

Baby elephants are never allowed to stray far from the herd and are fiercely protected by all its members. The adults are prone to intimidating displays of aggression towards intruders.

Overleaf: A group of eland, Africa's largest antelope, gathers to drink at a water point. Water is not essential for these arid-adapted animals provided there is a ready supply of succulent plant food available.

Previous page: Burchell's zebra slake their thirst in tidy formation.

Above: The solitary leopard – shy , elusive and among the most beautiful of carnivores.

A young lion, at rest in the long grass, is
interested in but wary of the camera.

*Overleaf: Majestic elephants take precedence
over zebra, giraffe and kudu at the waterbody.*

Previous page: Two of Africa's big cats, the lion (left) and the cheetah (right), savour the spoils of the hunt.

Opposite: Among Etosha's many different bird species are (left to right) the Pale Chanting Goshawk, the Lesser Flamingo and the Swallowtailed Bee-eater.

Above: A male Bateleur settles alongside the water. Although still found in numbers within the reserves, these strikingly coloured eagles are at risk beyond the safe confines of protected areas, and are generally far less common than they were at one time.

Overleaf: Ostriches on the edge of Etosha Pan.

Left: The black rhino, invincibly solid though it appears, is highly vulnerable to the poacher's bullet. There has been a dramatic decline in its overall numbers over the past three decades, and the species is now seriously endangered.

Above: A rock monitor, or leguaan – at the other end of the size spectrum from the massive rhino, but in its own distinctive way just as sturdy and imposing.

Previous page: The scorched bed of Etosha Pan, cracked and salt-encrusted during the colder, dry months.

Left: In years of good rain the usually desiccated surface of the pan is transformed into a shallow lake, attracting flocks of Greater and Lesser flamingoes. The birds arrive in their thousands, creating a beautiful spectacle of muted pinks and creams.

Overleaf, left: A spotted hyaena immerses itself in the cooling waters of a rain-filled pool.

Overleaf, right: A stand of bizarre moringa trees in the 'Enchanted Forest', part of the mopane woodland north-west of Okaukuejo.

Left: A bat-eared fox tilts its ears downwards in an effort to detect the underground movements of its insect prey.

Right: A black-faced impala herd timidly keeps to the edge of the waterhole, allowing the elephants to monopolize the main waterbody.

Overleaf: Dawn in the desert. These lions are preparing to rest after the night's hunt.

Previous page: Two young cheetahs explore the stark white salt formations along the edge of Etosha Pan.

Right: Elephants must drink daily to survive; an adult takes up to 200 litres in one session.

Overleaf (from left to right): Male lion; ground squirrel; red hartebeest.

Left: Elephant bulls are for the most part solitary animals, joining a herd only when a cow comes into oestrus.

Overleaf: A lone wildebeest feasts on the rich green pastures which emerge after rain.

51

Previous page: Helmeted Guineafowl (left), dwarfed by the park's giants; female lions (right) caught in restful pose.

Nocturnal foragers: both the scrub hare (above) and Cape fox (right) rest up during the long, hot daytime hours to conserve energy for the coming night's activity.

Overleaf: A young leopard crouches low to the ground to drink the fresh, sweet rainwater from a temporary pool.

A blackbacked jackal mother stands patiently to allow her pups to drink her milk. After an initial suckling period, the young are fed on regurgitated food, and then, at about three months of age, join their parents in foraging.

The wet season in Etosha heralds luxuriant
growth, the arrival of migrant birds and the
dropping of young, such as this springbok lamb.

The diminutive Damara dik-dik, common along the famed 'Dik-dik Drive' near Namutoni.

Overleaf: Blue wildebeest on the move.

Left: Gemsbok are capable of surviving without a regular supply of water. When available, however, water is readily taken.

Right: A stately kudu bull shows its elegantly spiralled horns and distinctive patterning as it stoops to drink.

An awkward and ungainly tangle between two springbok rams. During the rut, males defend their breeding territories and engage in frequent sparring matches, which more commonly involve the head and horns.

Left: A blackbacked jackal in serene mood. These opportunistic little carnivores are frequently seen busily weaving their way across the plains in Etosha.

Right: The haughty and imperious cheetah, fastest of all land mammals.

Overleaf: An elephant takes its time to complete the bathing ritual, oblivious of other animals standing in wait.

Gemsbok, true dwellers of the desert, are common residents of Etosha. Here, a large herd gathers at Fischer's Pan.

75

Waterholes are invariably well patronized in the hot, dry Etosha landscapes, and visitors to the park are assured of seeing a succession of different animals take their places at these prime viewing spots. Here, an impala ram and two giraffe quench their thirst.

Overleaf: Giraffes silhouetted against the gathering storm clouds in the fading sunlight of an Etosha landscape.

Ostriches pick up pace across the flooded pan surface, making their way to the centre where they will spend the night safe from predators.